M000232204

LENNON'S
LIFE
LESS ORDINARY

Published by OH!
20 Mortimer Street
London W1T 3JW

Disclaimer:
All trademarks, quotations, company names, registered names, individual names, products, logos and catchphrases used or cited in this book are the property of their respective owners and used in this book for informational, reporting, review and guidance purposes only. This book is a publication of *OH! An imprint of Welbeck Publishing Group Limited* and has not been licensed, approved, sponsored, or endorsed by any person or entity.

ISBN 978-1-91161-062-5

Compiled by: Malcolm Croft
Editorial: Stella Caldwell, Victoria Godden
Project manager: Russell Porter
Design: Andy Jones
Production: Rachel Burgess

A CIP catalogue record for this book is available from the British Library

Printed in Dubai

10 9 8 7 6 5 4 3 2 1

Jacket cover photograph: Everett Collection Inc/Alamy Stock Photo

THE LITTLE GUIDE TO
JOHN LENNON

LENNON'S LIFE LESS ORDINARY

CONTENTS

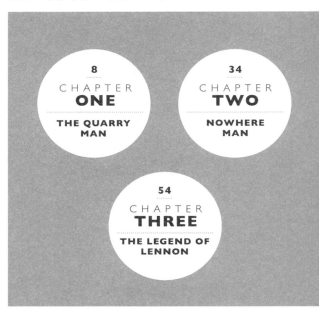

INTRODUCTION

John Lennon hasn't needed an introduction to anyone anywhere in the known universe since the early 1960s. But to not preface this icon here would be to betray the cultural importance of his incredible – incomparable – accomplishments, as both a songwriter and the chief cultural spokesperson for world peace. Lennon, ironically, is as close to divine as a rock 'n' roller can get.

Today, 40 years after his senseless murder, the word "Lennon" is synonymous with "legend". And while the world still struggles with the aftermath of losing someone so meaningful so meaninglessly, Lennon's legacy remains as deep-rooted as ever. He was a genius with words. "He had the quickest wit," McCartney said of his partner. "He was the smartest Beatle." Indeed, Lennon could cleverly turn any phrase on its head and eviscerate any pundit or presenter with quips and wisecracks that would spin the world inside out. His lyrics, both solo and with the

Beatles, were unquestionably the mark of a man both in pain and at the top of his game. But it was his wit and his wisdom away from the recording studio – and the pure conviction of those words – that ensured Lennon's memory will never fade.

Lennon's Life Less Ordinary: The Little Guide to John Lennon is a tiny tome that no home should be without. The songwriter, rock-star philanthropist and philosopher – and all-round quote machine – was rarely speechless; he was the gift that kept on giving. If only he had survived that terrible day on 8 December 1980, Lennon would no doubt still be raging against the machine and squeezing out even more nuggets of knowledge about peace, love and understanding. However, as his death ultimately proved, Lennon's universal gift for words of purpose and passion transcended time. And in the end, he did became more popular than Jesus, if only in terms of album sales. Imagine that.

Enjoy!

CHAPTER

ONE

THE QUARRY MAN

When the Quarry Men stepped on stage at the Woolton Parish school fete at 6.48pm on 6 July 1957, little did the teenage frontman, John Lennon, understand its significance. Little too did he know that in just a few short years, that formative band's name would come to hold such importance: Quarry Men, creatures to be hunted.

With Beatlemania in full swing, that's precisely how John and the rest of the group appeared to the world: prey. Picture yourself on a boat on a river, and let's take a trip down to Penny Lane's sister, Memory, and reminisce about how, when and why Lennon's Quarry Men kickstarted a revolution.

I've always considered my work one piece, and I consider that my work won't be finished until I am dead and buried and I hope that's a long, long time.

Lennon discussing his legacy while being interviewed on RKO Radio, 8 December 1980, (the day he was murdered).

As seen on *beatlesarchive.net*, 21 December 2013

66

I've been shot, I've been shot.

99

**Lennon's last words after being gunned down
by Mark Chapman, a crazed fan, in the doorway
of the Dakota Building, Lennon's New York
residence, at 10.50pm on 8 December 1980.
Lennon was shot five times and died almost
immediately.**

As seen on *NME.com*, 8 December 2000

"

Christianity will go. It will vanish and shrink. I needn't argue about that; I'm right and I'll be proved right. We're more popular than Jesus now; I don't know which will go first – rock 'n' roll or Christianity. Jesus was all right but his disciples were thick and ordinary. It's them twisting it that ruins it for me.

"

Maureen Cleaver's infamous interview with Lennon appeared in the *Evening Standard* on 4 March 1966 under the heading, "On a hill in Surrey… A young man, famous, loaded, and waiting for something". It wasn't until the article was reprinted in the American teen magazine *Datebook* on 29 July 1966 that chaos ensued. Lennon later apologized, claiming, "If I'd said, 'Television is more popular than Jesus,' I might have got away with it!"

As seen on *rollingstone.com,* 29 July 2016, by Jordan Runtaugh

---

If I'd had a better education, I wouldn't have been me. When I was at grammar school I thought I'd go to university, but I didn't get any GCEs. Then I went to art school and thought I'd go to the Slade and become a wonder. But I never fitted in. I was always a freak, I was never lovable. I was always Lennon!

Lennon discussing his education in an interview with friend and journalist Ray Connelly.

As seen on *thetimes.co.uk*, 25 July 2014, by Ray Connelly

I'm not claiming divinity. I've never claimed purity of soul. I've never claimed to have the answers to life. I only put out songs and answer questions as honestly as I can. But I still believe in peace, love and understanding.

Lennon discussing peace, love and understanding in an interview with *Playboy* conducted by David Sheff, published January 1981.

As seen on *npr.org*, posted 8 October 2010

It's just natural, it's not a great disaster. People keep talking about it like it's The End of The Earth. It's only a rock group that split up, it's nothing important. You know, you have all the old records there if you want to reminisce.

Lennon discussing the break-up of the Beatles in an interview in *Scene And Heard* conducted by David Wigg, 25 October 1971.

As seen on *irishtimes.com*, 16 September 2000, by Brian Boyd

We live in a world where we have to hide to make love, while violence is practised in broad daylight.

Lennon talking about the 1970s and the Vietnam War.

As seen on *irishpost.com*, October 2009, by Jack Beresford

When we say 'War is over if you want it,' we mean that if everyone demanded peace instead of another TV set, we'd have peace.

Lennon discussing peace during the infamous *Bed-In for Peace* in Montreal, Canada, 1 June 1969.

As seen on *independent.co.uk*, 8 December 2016, by Clarisse Loughrey

I brought Paul into the original group, the Quarry Men, he brought George in, and George brought Ringo in. And the second person who interested me as an artist and somebody I could work with was Yoko Ono. That ain't bad picking.

Lennon discussing the early Beatles formation in an interview with *Rolling Stone*.

As seen on *rollingstone.com*, 23 December 2010, by Jonathan Cott

I've got used to the fact – just about – that whatever I do is going to be compared to the other Beatles. If I took up ballet dancing, my ballet dancing would be compared with Paul's bowling.

Lennon discussing comparisons to his former bandmates in a 1975 interview with *Rolling Stone*.

As seen on *eu.usatoday.com*, 9 October 2017, by Elysa Gardner

I believe in God, but not as one thing, not as an old man in the sky. I believe that what people call God is something in all of us. I believe that what Jesus and Mohammed and Buddha and all the rest said was right. It's just that the translations have gone wrong.

Lennon's statement to reporters at O'Hare Airport in Chicago, 11 August 1966, following the fallout of his "We're more popular than Jesus" comment a few months earlier.

As seen on *irishpost.com*, October 2009, by Jack Beresford

We're trying to sell peace, like a product, you know, and sell it like people sell soap or soft drinks. And it's the only way to get people aware that peace is possible, and it isn't just inevitable to have violence. Not just war — all forms of violence.

Lennon discussing peace and love during an interview on *The David Frost Show*, 14 June 1969.

As seen in *Frost: That Was The Life That Was: The Authorized Biography* by Neil Hegarty

I've always thought there was this underlying thing in Paul's 'Get Back'. When we were in the studio recording it, every time he sang the line 'Get back to where you once belonged,' he'd look at Yoko.

Lennon discussing Yoko Ono's treatment by the group in an interview with *Playboy*, by David Sheff, September 1980 (published January 1981).

As seen on *usatoday.com*, 9 October 2015, by Elysa Gardner

"

I'm prepared for death because
I don't believe in it. I think it's just
getting out of one car and getting
into another.

"

**Lennon talking about religion and the afterlife,
with Yoko Ono, in an interview with David Wigg
at the Apple Offices, London, 8 May 1969.**

As seen on *beatlesinterviews.org*

We've got this gift of love, but love is like a precious plant… You've got to keep watering it. You've got to really look after it and nurture it.

Lennon discussing love during a "Man of the Decade" interview filmed by ATV, 2 December 1969.

As seen on *independent.com*, 8 December 2016, by Clarissa Loughrey

My role in society, or any artist or poet's role, is to try and express what we all feel. Not to tell people how to feel. Not as a preacher, not as a leader, but as a reflection of us all.

Lennon discussing his role in society in an interview with KFRC RKO Radio, 8 December 1980, the day he was murdered.

As heard on *openculture.com*, posted 12 March 2015

We're not Beatles to each other, you know. It's a joke to us. If we're going out the door of the hotel, we say, 'Right! Beatle John! Beatle George, now! Come on, let's go!' We don't put on a false front or anything.

Lennon talking about the Beatles, *Look* magazine, 13 December 1966.

As seen on *eu.usatoday.com*, 9 October 2015, by Elysa Gardner

Paul and I made a deal when we were 15. There was never a legal deal between us, just a deal we made when we decided to write together that we put both our names on it, no matter what.

Lennon talking about Lennon–McCartney songwriting in an interview with *Playboy*, by David Sheff, September 1980 (published January 1981).

As seen on *eu.usatoday.com*, 9 October 2015, by Elysa Gardner

We were really professional by the time we got to the States; we had learned the whole game. When we arrived here we knew how to handle the press; the British press were the toughest in the world and we could handle anything. We were all right.

Lennon talking about the Beatles in an interview conducted by *Rolling Stone* founder Jann S. Wenner, titled "Lennon Remembers".

As seen on *rollingstone.com*, 21 January 1971, by Jann S. Wenner

We're all God. I'm not a god
or the God, but we're all God
and we're all potentially divine –
and potentially evil. We all have
everything within us and the
Kingdom of Heaven is nigh and
within us, and if you look hard
enough you'll see it.

**Lennon talking about religion with Yoko Ono,
in an interview with David Wigg at the Apple
Offices, London, 8 May 1969.**

As seen on *beatlesinterviews.org*

They've been trying to knock us down since we began, especially the British press, always saying, 'What are you going to do when the bubble bursts?'… We'd go when we decided, not when some fickle public decided, because we were not a manufactured group. We knew what we were doing.

Lennon talking about the Beatles in an interview conducted by *Rolling Stone* founder Jann S. Wenner, titled "Lennon Remembers".

As seen on *rollingstone.com*, 21 January 1971, by Jann S. Wenner

When it gets down to having to use violence, then you are playing the system's game. The establishment will irritate you – pull your beard, flick your face – to make you fight. Because once they've got you violent, then they know how to handle you. The only thing they don't know how to handle is non-violence and humour.

Lennon discussing peace during the infamous _Bed-In for Peace_ in Montreal, Canada, 1 June 1969.

As seen on _independent.co.uk_, 8 December 2016

I am returning this MBE in protest against Britain's involvement in the Nigeria-Biafra thing, against our support of America in Vietnam and against 'Cold Turkey' slipping down the charts.

Lennon's letter to Queen Elizabeth II, sent in November 1969, along with the return of his MBE.

CHAPTER

TWO

NOWHERE MAN

To his legions of fans, John Lennon was always more than a mere mortal. To himself, however, he was as much a Nowhere Man as he was a Renaissance Man. "The cocky rock and roll hero who knows all the answers was actually a terrified guy who didn't know how to cry," Lennon said in 1969.

After the Beatles broke up, and driven by his teenage tragedies, Lennon spent his final decade on Earth searching for, and perhaps finding out, who he really was.

Come and have a feel.

Lennon quipping to an American press reporter's question "Are you for real?" at their infamous JFK Airport Press Conference, 7 February 1964.

As seen on *dmbeatles.com*

"If we knew, we'd form another group and be managers. "

Lennon quipping to an American press reporter's question "What excites your fans so much?" at their infamous JFK Airport Press Conference, 7 February 1964.

As seen on *dmbeatles.com*

We're money-makers first; then
we're entertainers.

**Lennon discusses the Beatles as commodities
in an interview with Jean Shepherd for *Playboy*
magazine, February 1965.**

As seen on *absoluteelsewhere. net*

When I first got out of the Beatles, I thought, 'Oh great. I don't have to listen to Paul and Ringo and George.' But it's boring yodelling by yourself in a studio.

Lennon discusses the break-up of the Beatles and his return to music in an interview with *Newsweek*'s Barbara Graustark, 29 September 1980.

As seen on *videomusic.eu*, 19 April 2018

Last Christmas our neighbours showed Sean *Yellow Submarine* and he came running in, saying, 'Daddy, you were singing… were you a Beatle?' He's not accustomed to it – in five years I hardly picked up a guitar.

Lennon discusses his house husbandry following the birth of his son, Sean, in an interview with *Newsweek*'s Barbara Graustark, 29 September 1980.

As seen on *videomusic.eu*, 19 April 2018

I hope we're a nice old couple
living off the coast of Ireland or
something like that – looking at our
scrapbook of madness.

**Lennon imagines the future with Yoko
and being aged 64 in an interview conducted
by *Rolling Stone* founder Jann S. Wenner, titled
"Lennon Remembers".**

As seen on *rollingstone.com*, 21 January 1971, by Jann S. Wenner

Come and stay. I'll put the gorilla suit on and we'll go for a drive in the Ferrari…

Lennon, inviting journalist Maureen Cleave to stay at his house, as remembered by Maureen Cleave. Lennon owned a gorilla suit.

As seen on *telegraph.co.uk*, 14 December 2009

I don't have any romanticism about any part of my past. I think of it only inasmuch as it gave me pleasure or helped me grow psychologically. That is the only thing that interests me about yesterday. I don't believe in yesterday, by the way. You know I don't believe in yesterday. I am only interested in what I am doing now.

Lennon discussing his legacy in an interview with *Playboy* conducted by David Sheff, 1981.

As seen on *npr.org*, posted 8 October 2010

It's nice to be able to read and write, but apart from that I never learned anything worth a damn, you know.

Lennon discussing his time at school, when interviewed by ATV for their "Man of the Decade", 2 December 1969.

As seen on *dmbeatles.com* and *youtube.com*

There is not one thing that's
Beatle music. How can they talk
about it like that? What is Beatle
music? 'Walrus' or 'Penny Lane'?
Which? It's too diverse: 'I Want
to Hold Your Hand' or 'Revolution
Number Nine'?

**Lennon talking about the Beatles in an
interview conducted by *Rolling Stone* founder
Jann S. Wenner, titled "Lennon Remembers".**

As seen on *rollingstone.com*, 21 January 1971, by Jann S. Wenner

Why should the Beatles give more?
Didn't they give everything on
God's Earth for ten years? Didn't
they give themselves?

**Lennon talking about the Beatles myth
in an interview with *Playboy*, by David Sheff,
September 1980 (published January 1981).**

As seen on *eu.usatoday.com*, 9 October 2015,
by Elysa Gardner

"

I said to Paul 'I'm leaving. I want a divorce.'

"

Lennon talking about the Beatles in an interview conducted by *Rolling Stone* founder Jann S. Wenner, titled "Lennon Remembers".

As seen on *rollingstone.com*, 21 January 1971, by Jann S. Wenner

My thing is, out of sight, out of mind. That's my attitude toward life. So I don't have any romanticism about any part of my past.

Lennon talking about his past life as a Beatle in an interview with *Playboy*, by David Sheff, September 1980 (published January 1981).

As seen on *eu.usatoday.com*, 9 October 2015, by Elysa Gardner

"

Nobody controls me. I'm uncontrollable. The only one who controls me is me, and that's just barely possible.

"

Lennon discussing his freedom of expression in an interview with *Playboy*, by David Sheff, September 1980 (published January 1981).

As seen on *eu.usatoday.com*, 9 October 2015, by Elysa Gardner

"

She inspired all this creation in me. It wasn't that she inspired the songs; she inspired me.

"

Lennon discussing Yoko's inspiration, in an interview with *Playboy*, by David Sheff, September 1980 (published January 1981).

As seen on *eu.usatoday.com*, 9 October 2015, by Elysa Gardner

It is a teacher–pupil relationship. That's what people don't understand. She's the teacher and I'm the pupil. I'm the famous one, the one who's supposed to know everything, but she's my teacher.

Lennon discussing Yoko's influence on him, in an interview with *Playboy*, by David Sheff, September 1980 (published January 1981).

As seen on *eu.usatoday.com*, 9 October 2015, by Elysa Gardner

One has to completely humiliate oneself to be what the Beatles were, and that's what I resent… It happened bit by bit, gradually, until this complete craziness is surrounding you, and you're doing exactly what you don't want to do with people you can't stand.

Lennon discussing the breakup of the Beatles in an interview conducted by Jann S. Wenner, titled "Lennon Remembers".

As seen on *rollingstone.com*, 21 January 1971

It looks like I'm going to be 40 and life begins at 40 – so they promise. And I believe it, too.

Lennon discusses the importance of self-belief, in an interview with *Playboy*, by David Sheff, September 1980 (published January 1981). He was dead three months later.

As seen on *eu.usatoday.com*, 9 October 2015, by Elysa Gardner

THREE

THE LEGEND OF LENNON

Following the later-era Beatles "freak show", as Lennon denounced it, the songwriter diverted his life away from the mainstream and dived headfirst into the avant-garde, a culture exploding with experimental art-rock, bagism, bed-ins, primal screams and free political expression.

Here, Lennon was reborn, transforming from a mortal rock god into a full-time philosopher – and thus the legend of Lennon came to be.

Part of me suspects that I'm a loser and the other part of me thinks I'm God Almighty.

Lennon discussing his legacy in an interview with *Playboy* conducted by David Sheff, published January 1981.

As seen on *npr.org*, posted 8 October 2010

It's better to fade away like an old soldier than to burn out. I don't believe in dead heroes. I don't appreciate worship of dead Sid Vicious, or of dead James Dean, or of dead John Wayne… I worship the people who survive.

As seen on *thetimes.co.uk*, 25 July 2014, by Ray Connelly

Only looks like one man to me…
Oh, it's the cameraman.

**Lennon's famous quip to a reporter who
asked Lennon to "speak to the American public,
40 million viewers" watching on television
in the US.**

As seen on *ranker.com*, 10 March 2017, by Katia Kleyman

They were playing 'All You Need is Love' earlier on the radio and I was saying to Yoko, 'I still believe all you need is love, you know.' But I don't believe that just saying it is going to do it, you know.

Lennon reflecting on Beatles songs in interviews conducted by Howard Smith between 1969–71, for *Blank on Blank*.

As seen on *rollingstone.com*, 22 April 2014, by Kory Grow

You don't need anybody to tell you who you are or what you are. You are what you are!

Lennon and Yoko discussing the release of the Plastic Ono Band's single "Give Peace a Chance" in a statement to the press, July 1969.

As seen on *beatlesbible.com*

It wasn't like 'You have to have peace!' Just give it a chance. We ain't giving any gospel here – just saying how about this version for a change? We think we have the right to have a say in the future. And we think the future is made in your mind.

Lennon discussing "Give Peace a Chance" with *Playboy*, in an interview conducted by David Sheff, published January 1981.

As seen on *npr.org*, posted 8 October 2010

"

I had a vision when I was 12,
and I saw a man on a flaming pie,
and he said, 'You are Beatles
with an A.' And so we are.

"

**Lennon revealing how the name the Beatles
was born, while promoting _Meet the Beatles!_ in
an interview conducted on 20 January 1964.**

As seen on _dmbeatles.com_

I have to see the others to
see myself.

**Lennon discussing his intimate
relationships with his bandmates, as quoted in
The Beatles Way: Fab Wisdom for Everyday Life
by Larry Lange.**

America — it just seemed ridiculous… I mean, the idea of having a hit record over there. It was just, you know, something you could never do. That's what I thought anyhow. But then I realized that it's just the same as in Britain, that kids everywhere all go for the same stuff.

Lennon discusses the Beatles' success in the US in an interview with Jean Shepherd for *Playboy* magazine, February 1965.

We used the Monkees on a few tracks.

Lennon quips about additional musicians performing on *Sgt. Pepper's Lonely Hearts Club Band* in an interview with Brian Matthew for BBC Radio, 20 March 1967.

As seen on *dmbeatles.com*

My mother was killed by an off-duty cop who was drunk. The underlying chip on my shoulder that I had as a youth got *really* big then. Being a teenager and a rock 'n' roller *and* an art student *and* my mother being killed just when I was re-establishing a relationship with her was *very* traumatic for me.

Lennon discussing his life in an interview with *Playboy* conducted by David Sheff, January 1981.

As seen on *npr.org*, posted 8 October 2010

Well, we're hustlin' peace,
that's all we do. We hustle for
peace. We can't see any other
way you know.

**Lennon discussing peace in an interview with
Hit Parade's Richard Robinson, August 1970.**

As seen on *instantkarma.com*

"

If we make peace trendy for six
months that'll give us enough
energy to carry on.

"

**Lennon discussing peace in an interview
with *Hit Parade*'s Richard Robinson,
August 1970.**

As seen on *instantkarma.com*

66

It's like saying, you know, 'Did you remember falling in love?' Not quite. It just sort of happens.

99

Lennon discussing the break-up of the Beatles on *The Dick Cavett Show*, 1971.

As seen on *eu.usatoday.com*, 9 October 2015, by Elysa Gardner

66

I was trying to write about an affair without letting my wife know I was writing about an affair, so it was very gobbledegook. I was sort of writing from my experiences, girls' flats, things like that.

99

Lennon on writing "Norwegian Wood" in an interview conducted by *Rolling Stone* founder, Jann S. Wenner, titled "Lennon Remembers".

As seen on *rollingstone.com*, 21 January 1971, by Jann S. Wenner

I believe Jesus was right, Buddha was right, and all of those people like that are right. They're all saying the same thing — and I believe it. I believe what Jesus actually said — the basic things he laid down about love and goodness — and not what people say he said.

Lennon talking about religion, in an interview with *Look* magazine, 13 December 1966.

As seen on *eu.usatoday.com*, 9 October 2015, by Elysa Gardner

We were smoking marijuana for breakfast. We were well into marijuana and nobody could communicate with us, because we were just all glazed eyes, giggling all the time. In our own world.

Lennon discussing the Beatles' marijuana days in an interview conducted by *Rolling Stone* founder, Jann S. Wenner, titled "Lennon Remembers".

As seen on *independent.co.uk*, 22 February 2020, by Mark Beaumont

You don't have to be a star to get
a cheese sandwich. You just have to
be first.

Lennon talking about fame (and food), *Look*
magazine, 13 December 1966.

As seen on *eu.usatoday.com*, 9 October 2015,
by Elysa Gardner

"

It's quite possible to do anything. Don't expect Jimmy Carter or Ronald Reagan or John Lennon or Yoko Ono or Bob Dylan or Jesus Christ to come and do it for you. You have to do it yourself.

"

Lennon discusses the importance of self-belief in an interview with *Playboy*, by David Sheff, September 1980 (published January 1981).

As seen on *eu.usatoday.com*, 9 October 2015, by Elysa Gardner

Here I am now, how are you?
How's your relationship going? Did
you get through it all? Weren't the
seventies a drag? Here we are, well,
let's try to make the eighties good,
because it's still up to us to make
what we can of it.

**Lennon discussing *Double Fantasy* at ROK Radio
on 8 December 1980, the day he died.**

As seen on *johnlennon.com*

The first line of 'I Am the Walrus' was written on one acid trip one weekend. The second line was written on the next acid trip the next weekend, and it was filled in after I met Yoko.

Lennon talking about "I Am the Walrus" in an interview with *Playboy*, by David Sheff, September 1980 (published January 1981).

As seen on *eu.usatoday.com*, 9 October 2015, by Elysa Gardner

They can take anything apart.
I hit it on all levels, you know.
We write lyrics, and I write lyrics
that you don't realize what they
mean till after.

**Lennon discussing fans (over-) analyzing
Beatles lyrics in an interview with *Rolling Stone*,
conducted by Jonathan Cott, 23 November
1968.**

As seen on *rollingstone.com*, 23 November 1968

You can be big-headed and say, 'Yeah, we're gonna last ten years.' But as soon as you've said that you think, 'We're lucky if we last three months,' you know.

Lennon pondering the Beatles' past, present and future, and responding to a reporter's question of "How long are you gonna last?" at a press conference in Manchester Dressing Room, 28 August 1963. The interview was filmed by the BBC for a programme entitled *The Mersey Sound.*

As seen on *dmbeatles.com*

"

Beatles are really the only people
who can play Beatle music.

"

**Lennon discusses the Beatles process in
an interview with *Flip* magazine, 15 May 1966.**

As seen on *dmbeatles.com*

Life doesn't end when you stop subscribing to *Billboard*.

Lennon discusses his five-year hiatus from music after *Walls & Bridges* (1974) and his return with *Double Fantasy* (1980) shortly before he was killed, in an interview with *Newsweek*'s Barbara Graustark, 29 September 1980.

As seen on *videomuzic.eu*, 19 April 2018

About two years ago, Paul turned up at the door. I said, 'Look, do you mind ringing first? I've just had a hard day with the baby. I'm worn out and you're walking in with a damn guitar!'

Lennon discusses McCartney's desire to rebuild their partnership in an interview with *Newsweek*'s **Barbara Graustark, 29 September 1980.**

As seen on *videomuzic.eu*, 19 April 2018

Everywhere is somewhere.

**Lennon, in existential mode, in an
interview with Jonathan Cott for *Rolling Stone*,
23 November 1968.**

As seen on *rollingstone.com*

There is no great mysterious meaning behind all of this; it was just four boys working out what to call a new album.

Lennon discussing the meaning behind the album title *Rubber Soul*, in an audio interview with Jann Wenner for *Rolling Stone*, December 1970.

As seen on *johnlennon.com*

FOUR

ENGLISHMAN IN NEW YORK

Liverpool and London may have housed Lennon during his Beatles days, but it was in the city that never sleeps, New York, that Lennon finally found himself at home, living in his two-storey mansion apartment on the northwest corner of 72nd Street and Central Park West in the Upper West Side of Manhattan.

"If I'd lived in Roman times, I'd have lived in Rome. Today, America is the Roman Empire, and New York is Rome itself. New York is the centre of the Earth," he was quoted as saying. He was finally granted residency in 1976. The journey home, however, was a long and winding road…

I'm always proud and pleased when people do my songs. It gives me pleasure that they even attempt them, because a lot of my songs aren't that doable.

Lennon talking about cover versions of his songs in an interview with *Playboy*, by David Sheff, September 1980 (published January 1981).

As seen on *eu.usatoday.com*, 9 October 2015, by Elysa Gardner

Yes, if there is such a thing as a genius, I am one. And if there isn't, I don't care.

Lennon on being a genius in an interview conducted by *Rolling Stone* founder Jann S. Wenner, titled "Lennon Remembers".

As seen on *rollingstone.com*, 21 January 1971, by Jann S. Wenner

One of my big things is that I wish to be a fisherman. I know it sounds silly — and I'd sooner be rich than poor, and all the rest of that… but I wish the pain was ignorance or bliss or something.

Lennon on ignorance being bliss in an interview conducted by *Rolling Stone* founder Jann S. Wenner, titled "Lennon Remembers".

As seen on *rollingstone.com*, 21 January 1971, by Jann S. Wenner

The thing the sixties did was to show us the possibilities and the responsibility that we all had. It wasn't the answer. It just gave us a glimpse of the possibility.

Lennon discussing the counter culturalism of the 1960s in an interview with KFRC RKO Radio (by Dave Sholin) on 8 December 1980, the day he died. It is known as the last interview Lennon ever gave.

As seen on *thenation.com*, 8 December 2010, by Jon Weiner

"

I couldn't hear the music for the
noise in my own head.

"

**Lennon discusses his five-year hiatus
from music, 1975–1980, in an interview with
Newsweek's Barbara Graustark,
29 September 1980.**

As seen on *videomuzic.eu*, 19 April 2018

I'm cynical about society, politics, newspapers, government.
But I'm not cynical about life, love, goodness, death. That's why I really don't want to be labelled a cynic.

Lennon talking about the state of the world, *Look* **magazine, 13 December 1966.**

As seen on *eu.usatoday.com*, 9 October 2015, by Elysa Gardner

When Yoko and I got married, we knew our honeymoon was going to be public… so we decided to use it to make a statement. We sat in bed and talked to reporters for seven days. It was hilarious… we were doing a commercial for peace on the front page of the papers instead of a commercial for war.

Lennon discussing his marriage and Bed-Ins for Peace, in an interview with *Playboy*, by David Sheff, September 1980 (published January 1981).

As seen on *eu.usatoday.com*, 9 October 2015, by Elysa Gardner

I was a working-class macho guy who was used to being served and Yoko didn't buy that. From the day I met her, she demanded equal time, equal space, equal rights.

Lennon discussing his relationship with Yoko in an interview with *Newsweek*, 1980.

As seen on *eu.usatoday.com*, 9 October 2015, by Elysa Gardner

I could still be forgotten when I'm dead. I don't really care what happens when I'm dead.

Lennon discussing his legacy on *The Dick Cavett Show*, 1971.

As seen on *eu.usatoday.com*, 9 October 2015, by Elysa Gardner

I don't mind looking to the camera
— it's people that throw me.

**Lennon talking about paparazzi, *Look* magazine,
13 December 1966.**

As seen on *eu.usatoday.com*, 9 October 2015,
by Elysa Gardner

For our last number, I'd like to ask your help. Would the people in the cheaper seats clap your hands. And the rest of you, if you'll just rattle your jewellery.

Lennon's famous quip at the Royal Variety Performance at the Royal Albert Hall, (4 November 1963), attended by Queen Elizabeth, the Queen Mother, and Princess Margaret. The remark was greeted with relief by Brian Epstein, whom Lennon had told before their performance that he was actually going to ask the crowd to "rattle their fuckin' jewellery."

It was a load of rubbish.
It was like meeting Engelbert
Humperdinck.

**Lennon's remark some time later after
meeting Elvis Presley.**

As seen on *beatlesnews.com*, 31 August 2015, by Ivor Davies

"

What's bagism? It's like… a tag for what we all do, we're all in a bag, you know?

"

Lennon explaining bagism in an interview on *The David Frost Show*, 14 June 1969.

As seen in *Frost: That Was The Life That Was: The Authorized Biography* by Neil Hegarty

I'd like to say 'thank you' on behalf of the group and ourselves and I hope we passed the audition.

Lennon's famous outro to the Beatles' rooftop concert on 30 January 1969. The line also concludes the notorious *Let It Be* film.

As seen on *youtube.com*, posted 10 April 2012, by Jonathan Narciso

Yoko is as important to me as Paul and Dylan rolled into one. I don't think she will get recognition until she's dead.

Lennon discussing Yoko Ono in an interview conducted by _Rolling Stone_ founder Jann S. Wenner, titled "Lennon Remembers".

As seen on _ew.com_, 9 November 2016, by Mary Sollosi

Turn left at Greenland.

Lennon responding to a reporter's mock question of 'How did you find America?' from a famous scene of *A Hard Day's Night* (1964).

As seen on *ranker.com*, 10 March 2017, by Katia Kleyman

We turn into Beatles because
everybody looking at us sees the
Beatles. We're not the Beatles at all.
We're just us.

**Lennon discusses the Beatles in an interview for
Look magazine, 13 December 1966.**

As seen on *dmbeatles.com*

"

I'm not high-powered. I just sort of stand there and let things happen to me.

"

Lennon discusses his laziness in an interview with *NME's* Chris Hutchins, 11 March 1966.

As seen on *uncut.co.uk*, 5 August 2016, by Tom Pinnock

Paul was always gently coming up to Yoko and saying: 'Why don't you keep in the background a bit more?' I didn't know what was going on. It was going on behind my back.

Lennon discussing Yoko in an interview with Peter McCabe and Robert Schonfeld, 5 September 1971.

As seen on *geocities.com/wireless_machine*

I lived in the suburbs in a nice semi-detached place… not the poor slummy kind of image that was projected… Paul, George and Ringo… lived in government-subsidized houses. We owned our own house, had our own garden, and they didn't have anything like that. So I was a bit of a fruit compared to them.

Lennon discussing the Beatles in an interview with *Playboy* **conducted by David Sheff, published 1981.**

As seen on *npr.org*, posted 8 October 2010

I never forgave my aunt Mimi for not treating me like a fucking genius or whatever I was… Why didn't they put me in art school? Why didn't they train me? Why would they keep forcing me to be a fuckin' cowboy like the rest of them? I was different, I was always different. Why didn't anybody notice me.

Lennon talking about his early family life in an interview conducted by *Rolling Stone* founder Jann S. Wenner, titled "Lennon Remembers".

As seen on *rollingstone.com*, 21 January 1971, by Jann S. Wenner

If you know your history, it took Yoko and me a long time to have a live baby. And I wanted to give five solid years to Sean. I hadn't seen Julian, my first son, grow up at all. And now there's a 17-year-old man on the phone talking about motorbikes.

Lennon discussing his children in an interview with _Newsweek_, 1980.

As seen on _eu.usatoday.com_, 9 October 2015, by Elysa Gardner

There is nothing conceptually better than rock 'n' roll. No group, be it Beatles, Dylan or Stones, have ever improved on 'Whole Lot of Shaking' for my money. Or maybe I'm like our parents: that's my period and I dig it and I'll never leave it.

Lennon on his musical influences in an interview conducted by *Rolling Stone* founder Jann S. Wenner on 21 January 1971, titled "Lennon Remembers".

As seen on *rollingstone.com*

That radicalism of the 1970s was phoney, really, because it was out of guilt. I'd always felt guilty that I made money, so I had to give it away or lose it. I don't mean I was a hypocrite. When I believe, I believe right down to the roots.

Lennon discussing the 1970s in an interview with *Newsweek*, 1980.

As seen on *eu.usatoday.com*, 9 October 2015, by Elysa Gardner

CHAPTER

FIVE

BIGGER THAN JESUS

Singer. Songwriter. Dreamer. Poet.
Philosopher. Rockstar. Rebel. Genius.
Leader. These are just many of
the words thrown at the continuing
legacy of John Lennon.

Forty years after his death,
Lennon remains an icon of the
people for the people, the ultimate
thinking man's rock and roller, a
wit paralleled only by his wisdom, a
"loser" whose ideas about peace,
love and understanding would make
him bigger than Jesus — a truth that
ultimately led to his untimely death.
Read all about it…

There is no denying that we are still living in the capitalist world. I think that in order to survive and to change the world, you have to take care of yourself first. You have to survive yourself.

Lennon discusses the material world in an interview with *Playboy*, by David Sheff, September 1980 (published January 1981).

As seen on *eu.usatoday.com*, 9 October 2015, by Elysa Gardner

I couldn't think of the next few years; it's abysmal thinking of how many years there are to go, millions of them. I just play it week by week.

Lennon discussing the longevity of life in an interview conducted by *Rolling Stone* founder Jann S. Wenner on 21 January 1971, titled "Lennon Remembers".

As seen on *rollingstone.com*

"

Isn't it time we destroyed the macho ethic?… Where has it gotten us all of these thousands of years? Are we still going to have to be clubbing each other to death? Do I have to arm-wrestle you to have a relationship with you as another male?… Can we not have a relationship on some other level?

"

Lennon discussing the counter culturalism of the 1960s in an interview with KFRC RKO Radio, (by Dave Sholin), on 8 December 1980, the day he died.

As seen on *thenation.com*, 8 December 2010, by Jon Weiner

I feel I want to be them all — painter, writer, actor, singer, player, musician. I want to try them all, and I'm lucky enough to be able to. I want to see which one turns me on. Apart from wanting to do it all because of what it stands for, I want to see what I'll be like when I've done it all.

Lennon discusses his desire to be a multi-hyphenate creator in an interview for *Look* magazine, 13 December 1966.

As seen on *dmbeatles.com*

Paul and I wrote a lot of stuff together, one-on-one, eyeball to eyeball. Like in 'I Want To Hold Your Hand', I remember when we got the chord that made the song. We were in Jane Asher's house, downstairs in the cellar playing on the piano at the same time. And we had, 'Oh you-u-u… got that something…'

… And Paul hits this chord and I turn to him and say, 'That's it!' I said, 'Do that again!' In those days, we really used to absolutely write like that — both playing into each other's nose.

"

Lennon discussing the Lennon–McCartney partnership in an interview with *Playboy* conducted by David Sheff, published January 1981.

As seen on *beatlesbible.com*

Yoko changed my life completely.
Not just physically... the only way I
can describe it is that Yoko was like
an acid trip or the first time you
got drunk. It was that big a change,
and that's just about it. I can't
really describe it to this day. Her
influence is so overwhelming that it
was big enough not only for me to
change my life with the Beatles...

… but also my private life, which has nothing to do with how sexually attractive we are to each other.

Lennon discussing his love for Yoko in an interview with *NME*'s Roy Carr, 7 October 1972.

As seen on *instantkarma.com*

"

My name isn't John Beatle. It's John Lennon. Just like that.

"

Lennon discussing his post-Beatles identity in an interview conducted by *Rolling Stone* founder Jann S. Wenner on 21 January 1971, titled "Lennon Remembers".

As seen on *rollingstone.com*

Well, there was this Japanese monk. He was in love with this big golden temple, you know, he really dug it, like — and you know he was so in love with it, he burnt it down so that it would never deteriorate. That's what I did with the Beatles.

Lennon discussing the breakup of the Beatles in an interview with Alan Smith for *NME: At Home with the Lennons*, 7 August 1971.

As seen on *rocksbackpages.com*

I've always been politically minded, you know, and against the status quo… When I started, rock 'n' roll itself was the basic revolution to people of my age and situation. We needed something loud and clear to break through all the unfeeling and repression that had been coming down on us kids.

Lennon in an interview entitled "Lenin or Lennon?" with *The Red Mole*, first published in March 1971.

As seen on *redpepper.org*, 30 October 2014, by Robin Blackburn and Tariq Ali

Yoko became the breadwinner,
taking care of the bankers and deals.
And I became the housewife.
It was like one of those reversal
comedies! To all housewives, I say
I now understand what you're
screaming about.

**Lennon discussing his children in an interview
with *Newsweek*, 1980.**

As seen on *eu.usatoday.com*, 9 October 2015,
by Elysa Gardner

All music is rehash. There are only a few notes. Just variations on a theme. Try to tell the kids in the seventies who were screaming to the Bee Gees that their music was just the Beatles redone. There is nothing wrong with the Bee Gees.

Lennon discussing music in an interview with _Playboy_, by David Sheff, September 1980 (published January 1981).

As seen on _eu.usatoday.com_, 9 October 2015, by Elysa Gardner

I worked for money and I wanted to be rich. So what the hell — if that's a paradox, then I'm a socialist. But I am not anything. What I used to be is guilty about money. That's why I lost it, either by giving it away or by allowing myself to be screwed by so-called managers.

Lennon discussing his immense fortune in an interview with *Playboy* conducted by David Sheff, on 8 December 1980, the day he died, published January 1981.

As seen on *npr.org*, posted 8 October 2010

"

You have to be a bastard to make it, and that's a fact. And the Beatles are the biggest bastards on Earth.

"

Lennon discussing the breakup of the Beatles in an interview conducted by *Rolling Stone* founder Jann S. Wenner on 21 January 1971, titled "Lennon Remembers".

As seen on *rollingstone.com*

"

Art is only a way of
expressing pain.

,,

**Lennon discussing his art and songwriting
in an interview entitled "Lenin or Lennon?" with
The Red Mole, first published in March 1971.**

As seen on *redpepper.org*, 30 October, 2014, by Robin
Blackburn and Tariq Ali

They keep telling me I'm all right for money but then I think I may have spent it all by the time I'm 40 so I keep going. That's why I started selling my cars; then I changed my mind and got them all back and a new one too.

Lennon discussing his wealth in his infamous interview with Maureen Cleave in the *Evening Standard*, 4 March, 1966.

As seen on *beatlesbible.com*

We were four guys. I met Paul, and said, 'You want to join me band?' Then George joined and then Ringo joined. We were just a band that made it very, very big, that's all. Our best work was never recorded.

Lennon discussing the Beatles' success in an interview conducted by *Rolling Stone* founder Jann S. Wenner on 21 January 1971, titled "Lennon Remembers".

As seen on *rollingstone.com*

"

After Brian died, we collapsed. Paul took over and supposedly led us. But what is leading us, when we went round in circles? We broke up then. That was the disintegration.

"

Lennon discussing the Beatles following the death of Brian Epstein, in an interview conducted by *Rolling Stone* founder Jann S. Wenner on 21 January 1971, titled "Lennon Remembers".

As seen on *rollingstone.com*

Rock and roll will be whatever we make it.

Lennon discussing the Beatles in an audio interview with Jann Wenner for *Rolling Stone*, December 1970.

As seen on *johnlennon.com*

Famous and loaded as I am, I still have to meet soft people. It often comes into my mind that I'm not really rich. There are really rich people but I don't know where they are.

Lennon discussing his wealth in his infamous interview with Maureen Cleave in the *Evening Standard*, 4 March 1966.

As seen on *beatlesbible.com*

The youth of today are really looking for some answers – for proper answers the established Church can't give them, their parents can't give them, material things can't give them.

Lennon discussing the youth revolution of the 1960s on *The Frost Programme*, conducted by David Frost on 4 October 1967.

As seen on *youtube.com*

There's an old joke, but it's true:
Sometimes you'd get this girl after
a show and you'd be in bed and
she'd ask you which Beatle you
are. I'd say, 'Which one do you
like?' If she said, 'George,' I'd say,
'I'm George.'

**Lennon discussing the perks of fame in an 1980
interview with Robert Hilburn, as revealed in his
autobiography *Corn Flakes with John Lennon (and
Other Tales From a Rock 'n' Roll Life)*.**

As seen on *latimes.com*, 11 October 2009, by Robert Hilburn

I can knock the Beatles, but don't
let Mick Jagger knock them.

**Lennon discussing the Beatles in an audio
interview with Jann Wenner for *Rolling Stone*,
December 1970.**

As seen on *johnlennon.com*

I thought we were the best fucking
group in the goddamn world, and
believing that is what made us
what we were, whether you call
it the best pop group or the best
rock 'n' roll group or whatever.
As far as we were concerned, we
were the best, but we thought
we were the best before anybody
else had even heard of us, back in
Hamburg and Liverpool…

… So in that respect I think the Beatles are the best thing that ever happened in pop music, but you play me those tracks and I want to remake every damn one of them.

,,

Lennon discussing the Beatles in an interview with *Playboy* conducted by David Sheff, published January 1981.

As seen on *npr.org*, posted 8 October 2010

CHAPTER

SIX

WORKING-CLASS HERO

If "Ringo was the heart of the Beatles", as Lennon once claimed, and Paul was the head, and George was the soul — what body part belonged to Lennon? The feet? The arms?

No, Lennon was the hands that bound and sculpted all the other elements together, and made them operate as one. He gave them the first-of-a-kind fingerprint that gave the band their identity and distinguished them from all else.

This is the story of how that came to be, in Lennon's own words…

I've withdrawn many times. Part of me is a monk, and part a performing flea! The fear in the music business is that you don't exist if you're not at Xenon with Andy Warhol.

Lennon discussing the music industry in an interview with *Newsweek*, 1980.

As seen on *eu.usatoday.com*, 9 October 2015, by Elysa Gardner

Half the time you don't know what you're talking about when you're talking to reporters.

Lennon discussing his relationship with reporters on *The Dick Cavett Show*, 1971.

As seen on *eu.usatoday.com*, 9 October 2015, by Elysa Gardner

You're born in pain. Pain is what we are in most of the time, and I think that the bigger the pain, the more God you look for.

Lennon on religion in an interview conducted by *Rolling Stone* founder Jann S. Wenner on 21 January 1971, titled "Lennon Remembers".

As seen on *rollingstone.com*

The unknown is what it is. And
to be frightened of it is what
sends everybody scurrying around
chasing dreams, illusions, wars,
peace, love, hate, all that… it's
all illusion.

**Lennon discusses fear of the unknown
in an interview with *Playboy*, by David Sheff,
September 1980 (published January 1981).**

As seen on *eu.usatoday.com*, 9 October 2015,
by Elysa Gardner

I don't want to die, and I don't want to be hurt physically, but if they blow the world up… we're all out of our pain then, forget it, no more problems.

Lennon discussing war in an interview on 21 January 1971 conducted by *Rolling Stone* founder Jann S. Wenner, titled "Lennon Remembers".

As seen on *rollingstone.com*

Maybe in the sixties we were naive… everyone went back to their rooms and said, 'We didn't get a wonderful world of flowers and peace… The world is a nasty horrible place because it didn't give us everything we cried for.' Right? Crying for it wasn't enough.

Lennon discussing the failure of the 1960s peace movement in an interview with KFRC RKO Radio on 8 December 1980, the day he died. It is known as the last interview Lennon ever gave.

As seen on *thenation.com*, 8 December 2010, by Jon Weiner

I'm Eric.

**Lennon's famous quip to an American
reporter who asked him, "Which one are you?"
during a TV interview at the British Embassy
reception following their concert at the
Washington Coliseum, 11 February 1964.**

As seen on *ranker.com*, 10 March 2017, by Katia Kleyman

Our society is run by insane people for insane objectives… I think we're being run by maniacs for maniacal ends and I think I'm liable to be put away as insane for expressing that. That's what's insane about it.

Lennon discussing the insanity of the modern world.

As seen on *independent.co.uk*, 8 December 2016, by Clarisse Loughrey

I've had cocaine, but I don't like it.
The Beatles had lots of it in their
day, but it's a dumb drug, because
you have to have another one
20 minutes later. Your whole
concentration goes on getting the
next fix.

**Lennon discussing drugs in an interview
with *Playboy* conducted by David Sheff, on
8 December 1980, the day he died, published
January 1981.**

As seen on *npr.org*, posted 8 October 2010

What would you suggest I do?
Give everything away and walk the
streets? The Buddhist says, 'Get rid
of the possessions of the mind.'
Walking away from all the money
would not accomplish that. It's like
the Beatles. I couldn't walk away
from the Beatles.

Lennon discussing his immense fortune in an interview with *Playboy* conducted by David Sheff, on 8 December 1980, the day he died, published January 1981.

As seen on *npr.org*, posted 8 October 2010

I had to sack them. They were very nice and gentle, but they kept going around saying 'peace' all the time. It was driving me mad. I couldn't get any fucking peace.

Lennon discussing the Hare Krishnas that moved next to his Surrey estate when interviewed by ATV for their "Man of the Decade", 2 December 1969.

As seen on *thetimes.co.uk*, 25 July 2014, by Ray Connelly

I'm not going to waste my life as
I have been, which was running
at 20,000 miles an hour. I have
to learn not to do that, because
I don't want to die at forty.

As seen on *thetimes.co.uk*, 25 July 2014, by Ray Connelly

I go to restaurants and the groups always play 'Yesterday'. I even signed a guy's violin in Spain after he played us 'Yesterday'. He couldn't understand that I didn't write the song. But I guess he couldn't have gone from table to table playing 'I Am the Walrus'.

Lennon discussing his songwriting in an interview with *Playboy* conducted by David Sheff, on 8 December 1980, the day he died, published January 1981.

As seen on *npr.org*, posted 8 October 2010

I've never met anybody who's had a flashback in my life and I took millions of trips in the sixties, and I've never met anybody who had any problem. I've had bad trips, but I've had bad trips in real life. I've had a bad trip on a joint. I can get paranoid just sitting in a restaurant.

Lennon discussing drugs in an interview with _Playboy_ conducted by David Sheff, published January 1981.

As seen on _npr.org_, posted 8 October 2010

The whole thing died in my mind long before all the rumpus started. We used to believe the Beatles myth just as much as the public, and we were in love with them in just the same way. But basically we were four individuals who eventually recovered our own individualities after being submerged in a myth. I know a lot of people were upset when we finished, but every circus has to come to an end...

… The Beatles were a monument that had to be either changed or scrapped. As it happens, it was scrapped. The Beatles were supposed to be this and supposed to be that, but really all we were was a band that got very big. **"**

Lennon reminiscing to Ray Connolly about the break-up of the Beatles.

As seen on *thetimes.co.uk*, 25 July 2014, by Ray Connelly

Mick Jagger said we weren't a good band as performers. But he never saw us at our best in Liverpool and Hamburg. We were the best bloody band there was. I know all the early rock songs much better than most of those I've written myself.

Lennon speaking to Ray Connolly about the early days with the Beatles.
As seen on *thetimes.co.uk*, 25 July 2014, by Ray Connelly

Paul and me were the Beatles.
We wrote the songs.

**Lennon speaking to Ray Connolly about Paul
and their songwriting.**
As seen on *thetimes.co.uk*, 25 July 2014, by Ray Connelly

It was Yoko that changed me. She
forced me to become avant-garde
and take me clothes off when all
I wanted to do was become
Tom Jones. And now look at me!
Did you know avant-garde is
French for bullshit?

**Lennon in conversation with Ray Connolly
about the influence Yoko had on him in the early
days of their relationship.**
As seen on *thetimes.co.uk*, 25 July 2014, by Ray Connelly

It must be hell.

**Lennon's response when asked what it must
be like for Julian to have John Lennon as a
father in an interview conducted by Francis
Schoenberger, in spring 1975.**

As seen on *spin.com*, 9 October 2019, by Francis Schoenberger

I like people to like me. But I am not going to ruin my life to please anybody.

Lennon on his likeability in an interview conducted by Francis Schoenberger, in spring 1975.

As seen on *spin.com*, 9 October 2019, by Francis Schoenberger

I had all the biggest cars in the world… and I don't even like cars. I bought everything that I could buy. The only thing that I never got into is yachts. So, I went through that period. There is nothing else to do once you do it. I just live however makes me most comfortable.

Lennon on money in an interview conducted by Francis Schoenberger, in spring 1975.

As seen on *spin.com*, 9 October 2019, by Francis Schoenberger

It is a big apartment, and it's beautiful, but it doesn't have grounds… you know, it's secure. And people can't get in and say, 'I'm Jesus from Toronto,' and all that. That still happens. Which was happening in the other apartment. You just couldn't go out the front door, because there would be something weird at the door.

Lennon on his New York residence, the Dakota Building, in an interview conducted by Francis Schoenberger, in spring 1975.

As seen on *spin.com*, 9 October 2019, by Francis Schoenberger

I spent most of the time drunk on the floor… with Harry Nilsson and Ringo and people like that. And ending up in the papers… that went on for about nine months. It was just one big hangover. It was hell. But that's why I was there.

Lennon on his famous "Lost Weekend", following his separation from Yoko, in an interview conducted by Francis Schoenberger, in spring 1975.

As seen on *spin.com*, 9 October 2019, by Francis Schoenberger

"

Stay alive in '75. That's my motto.
I don't know. I just feel pretty
alright. '74 was just hell. Just a drag.
'74 lasted about three years…

"

**Lennon on his famous "Lost Weekend" in an
interview conducted by Francis Schoenberger, in
spring 1975.**

As seen on *spin.com*, 9 October 2019, by Francis Schoenberger

I got fat when we got rich
and famous.

**Lennon on his "fat Elvis" period in an interview
conducted by Francis Schoenberger, in spring
1975.**

As seen on *spin.com*, 9 October 2019, by Francis Schoenberger

The problem for me is that as I have become less real, I've grown away from most working-class people. It's the students who are buying us now, and that's the problem. Now the Beatles are four separate people, we don't have the impact we had when we were together.

Lennon discussing the origins of rock and roll in an interview entitled "Lenin or Lennon?" with *The Red Mole*, first published in March 1971.

As seen on *redpepper.org*, 30 October 2014, by Robin Blackburn and Tariq Ali

If Yoko took the Beatles apart, can we please give her credit for all the nice music that George made and Ringo made and Paul made and I've made since they broke up, if she did it? She didn't split the Beatles… The Beatles were drifting apart on their own.

Lennon discussing the break-up of the Beatles in an interview conducted by *Rolling Stone* founder Jann S. Wenner, titled "Lennon Remembers".

As seen on *ew.com*, 9 November 2016, by Mary Sollosi

> **"**
>
> Well, that's very observant of them, cause we aren't American, actually. **"**

Lennon's famous quip, during a 1963 press interview before the Beatles first came to America, to a reporter who said "The Americans think your haircuts are un-American."

I can't give you the formula for meeting the person that you're going to love, but it's around, you know. And it happens. It happened to me at 29 and Yoko Ono at 32.

Lennon discussing Yoko, in interviews conducted by Howard Smith between 1969 and 1971, for *Blank on Blank*.

As seen on *rollingstone.com*, 22 April 2014, by Kory Grow

It means Beatles, doesn't it?
That's just a name. You know,
like shoe.

**Lennon's response to a press reporter during
a 1964 interview who asked Lennon the
significance of the name Beatles.**

As seen on *ranker.com*, 10 March 2017, by Katia Kleyman

"

Rubbish. I'm contracted. I've been trying to get out for years.

"

Lennon's response to a press reporter during a 1965 interview who told the singer that there was a rumour in *The Beatles Paper* that he might be leaving the group.

As seen on *ranker.com*, 10 March 2017, by Katia Kleyman

We were manufacturing it. Business went bonkers.

Lennon, during an interview, when a reporter asked about their public endorsement of LSD.

As seen on *ranker.com*, 10 March 2017, by Katia Kleyman

Nothing will ever break the love we have for each other and I still believe all you need is love. I don't have to live with three guys to prove that love is the basic necessity of all of us, you know.

Lennon discussing his former bandmates in interviews conducted by Howard Smith between 1969 and 1971, for *Blank on Blank*.

As seen on *rollingstone.com*, 22 April 2014, by Kory Grow

❝

I want the money just to be rich.
If you have money, that's power
without having to be powerful. **❞**

**Lennon discussing his wealth in his infamous
interview with Maureen Cleave in the *Evening
Standard*, 4 March 1966.**

As seen on *beatlesbible.com*

Reality leaves a lot to the imagination.

Lennon discussing reality as remembered by friend and journalist Maureen Cleave.

As seen on *telegraph.com*, 14 December 2009, by Maureen Cleave

66

We've never had time before to
do anything but just be Beatles.

99

**Lennon discussing the Beatles in his infamous
interview with Maureen Cleave in the *Evening
Standard*, 4 March 1966.**

As seen on *beatlesbible.com*

The dream is over. I'm not just talking about the Beatles, I'm talking about the generation thing. It's over, and we gotta – I have to personally – get down to so-called reality.

Lennon discussing the break-up of the Beatles, and the 1960s, in an interview conducted by *Rolling Stone* founder Jann S. Wenner, titled "Lennon Remembers".

As seen on *rollingstone.com*, 21 January 1971, by Jann S. Wenner

We could split up in 1970 because we were on top. In fact, it was probably the best thing that ever happened to the Beatles myth.

Lennon discussing the Beatles myth in an 1980 interview with Robert Hilburn, as revealed in his autobiography _Corn Flakes with John Lennon (and Other Tales From a Rock 'n' Roll Life)._

As seen on _latimes.com_, 11 October 2009, by Robert Hilburn

'A Day in the Life Of', that was something. I dug it. It was a good piece of work between Paul and me. I had the 'I read the news today' bit, and it turned Paul on, because now and then we really turn each other on with a bit of song, and he just said 'yeah' – bang bang, like that.

Lennon discussing the Lennon–McCartney songwriting partnership in an interview with Jonathan Cott on 23 November 1968 for _Rolling Stone_.

As seen on _rollingstone.com_

When we hit town, we hit it.
There was no pissing about. There's
photographs of me crawling about
in Amsterdam on my knees coming
out of whore houses and things
like that.

**Lennon discussing the Beatles' early days,
in an audio interview with Jann Wenner for
Rolling Stone, December 1970.**

As seen on *johnlennon.com*

" There's no other time but the present. Anything else is a waste of time. **"**

Lennon discussing the importance of now, in an interview with *Melody Maker*'s Michael Watts, 2 October 1971.

As seen on *instantkarma.com*

"

I don't think that age really matters.
It's like a weather report.

"

**Lennon discussing ageing in a radio interview
on the Elliot Mintz programme and broadcast
first by radio station KLOS (95.5) FM,
10 October 1971.**

A Rolls, Mini and a Ferrari. The Mini for pottering about in, the Rolls for relaxing in, and the Ferrari for zoom. I do very little driving. I'm not a very good driver.

Lennon discussing his cars in an interview entitled "Why Does Mr Lennon Keep a Stone Frog?" for *Disc Weekly*, 26 March 1966, by Ray Coleman.

As seen on *kenwoodlennon.com*

I would have thought I've done more good for Britain than harm, wouldn't you?

Lennon discussing the backlash in Britain, following his move to New York, in an interview entitled *Please, Your Majesty, Can Our John Have A Free Pardon?* with *NME's* Andrew Tyler, 19 January 1974.

As seen on *rocksbackpages.com*

I was really drawn to the Goons.
In many ways they influenced the
Beatles as much as rock 'n' roll –
Elvis and Little Richard. They were,
to my generation, what we were
to the next.

**Lennon discussing his influences in an interview
entitled "Please, Your Majesty, Can Our John
Have a Free Pardon?" with *NME*'s Andrew Tyler,
19 January 1974.**

As seen on *rocksbackpages.com*

> **When you've seen one cock you've seen them all.**

Lennon discussing penises in an interview entitled "Please, Your Majesty, Can Our John Have a Free Pardon?" with *NME*'s Andrew Tyler, 19 January 1974.

As seen on *rocksbackpages.com*

I couldn't believe it. It was like an album coming out of the oven.

Lennon recalling baking his first loaf of bread, with son Sean, as a house husband in New York, in an interview with David Sheff for *Playboy*, published 1981.

As seen on *npr.org*, 8 October 2010, by David Sheff

It's the old story of never knowing how much money we've got. I've tried to find out, but with income tax to be deducted and the money coming in from all over the place, the sums get too complicated for me, I can't even do my times table.

Lennon discusses his new-found wealth in an interview with _NME_'s Chris Hutchins, 11 March 1966.

As seen on _uncut.co.uk_, 5 August 2016, by Tom Pinnock

JOHN LENNON

I was always waiting for a reason to get out of the Beatles from the day I filmed *How I Won The War* (in 1966). I just didn't have the guts to do it. The seed was planted when the Beatles stopped touring and I couldn't deal with not being on stage.

Lennon discusses the break-up of the Beatles in an interview with *Newsweek*'s Barbara Graustark, 29 September 1980.

As seen on *videomuzic.eu*, 19 April 2018

Whatever made the Beatles the Beatles also made the 60s the 60s. And anybody who thinks that if John and Paul got together with George and Ringo, the Beatles would exist, is out of their skulls. The Beatles gave everything they had to give, and more. The four guys who used to be that group can never ever be that group again even if they wanted to be. What if Paul and I got together?...

… It would be boring. Whether George or Ringo joined in is irrelevant because Paul and I created the music. OK? There are many Beatle tracks that I would redo – they were never the way I wanted them to be. But going back to the Beatles would be like going back to school… I was never one for reunions. It's all over.

Lennon nixes a Beatles reunion in an interview with *Newsweek*'s Barbara Graustark, 29 September 1980.

As seen on *videomuzic.eu*, 19 April 2018

We both had our fingers in each other's pies.

Lennon on the Lennon–McCartney songwriting partnership in an interview with Jann Wenner for *Rolling Stone*, 8 December 1970.

As seen on *rollingstone.com*, 19 May 2017